Lost & Found

Taher Adel

authorHOUSE®

AuthorHouse™ UK
1663 Liberty Drive
Bloomington, IN 47403 USA
www.authorhouse.co.uk
Phone: 0800.197.4150

Published by AuthorHouse 04/16/2018

ISBN: 978-1-5462-9154-1 (sc)
ISBN: 978-1-5462-9155-8 (e)

Print information available on the last page.

Contents

This book is dedicated to my Mother and Father, Muna and Adel.

Acknowledgements

A special thanks to the artists:

Amber McCoy – Candle Beauty(90), It is He (31), Nest of Hope (57), The Heir (84), Writing Another Page (27), Time Waits for Us to Meet (11)
Janko M – Worldly Imitation(126), Tale of the Sun and Moon (36)
Jim Burgman – Forever Destined (23)
Makhfud - Love at First Plight (136)
Taufik Istihar – Lost&Found (1)
Kelelowar – I Cannot Go To Sleep (101)
Nuran Kamal – The Beauty Of He (43)
Gilang Saputra – Taming My Demon (119)

Taher Adel's poetic journey started at the age of sixteen when he first learnt how to utilise poetry as an outlet for his reflective nature. This book is a compilation of selected poetry from the start of his poetic expedition until today. Each poem contained within 'Lost and Found' explores the process of self discovery through pure artistry and wisdom while gently wandering into the realms of the soul. His poetry embodies the relationship between a divine creator and his creation, taking the reader on a journey back and forth between despair and hope, life and death.

Lost & Found

Wade into every line of my poetry
Like walking through a lucid dream
Witness my soul slipping into the whiteness of the paper
Feel it struggling, see it sink
Watch it get lost then found by ink
See my journey trapped in rhyme
And see the scars frozen in time
With enough syllables to tangle a spider in its own web
Forever getting lost in the maze of the world
Forever finding my way back by
Tracing its spherical edges with words

Taher Adel
04/11/2017

God In Words

Everywhere I look, each path I take, each road I pass
I see the signs, perfectly designed
By the words of God
In gills that breathe ocean deep
And wings aloft like silken dreams
The scent of flowery beauteous worth
Inked upon the body of His earth
And when I gaze back into my eyes
I see two panels of stained glass
Inside, a thousand worlds wander by
Like leaves falling upon a winters sigh
A repetitive sunset in a summer sky
Against a backdrop of deep crimson silk
Upon spherical shores, seas of milk
My eyes
Tell a tale of a craftsman of superior skill
A hand precise, bringing fire to the minute details of noon
To the silver lines of a rising moon
Traced out upon galaxies in darkness lost
Birthing stars like breaths of autumn frost
Even in death, we see Him write
Just as He turns dark to light
To life from gloom
Then the promise of blossom
And flowers return to bloom

But the greatest miracle of them all
Is drawn out upon the tapestry of the soul
Woven by light and a breath of life
A bodiless form He placed inside
To move, to think, to love then die
So that He may yet ask
"Which of the signs of your Lord will you deny?" - 55:16

Taher Adel
14/05/2015

A Stranger

Here I am, standing before you
A stranger
Here I am, begging at your door
A stranger
While You see my same eyes
No stranger
Than the day I was born
From the first brick laid
Into this temporary world
The place I keep stacking my days
Into neatly folded piles
Some days clean and crisp
Without a stain
But others I would try to burn away
With all my sins
Sins I intend to bury
Somewhere where no man could ever find them
But all I could do is hide them
Until I stumble across them again
And unearth them like
Threads that have been carelessly woven
A plain tapestry of years and hidden memories
They are no longer air tight stitches
As they unfold and with them
The upholstery of my darkness

Blowing away the final candles
From guidance to blindness
And now I realise my days are worthless
And my secrets pointless
My sins are heavy
And I am nothing in this world
But a stranger
So what use do you have for this stranger?
Who has abandoned his purity
Forsaken your word
And allowed darkness to infiltrate his light
To the point where he only sees you on these rare nights
Using Your name to penetrate his sight
To eclipse the edges of his sin torn heart
Leaving him to chase but his chains are too heavy
And his soul wingless
But here he is, kneeling before you
Because his legs are too ashamed by the
days they have walked away from You
Here he is, begging at your door
Because he abandoned the wings you once gave him
And he can no longer fly over to your mercy
Here he is, the soul you named
Before his mother knew of him in her womb
Here he is, the life you whispered

Before his heart welcomed blood to its rooms
Here he is, with this same heart darkened and charred
Here he is, clinging on to the promise unearned
Here he is, the one You promised to
love if he loved You in turn
Here he is, ashamed, hopeful, and concerned
Hoping that you will take back an old friend
Here he is, a stranger
Who is tired of being a stranger.

Taher Adel
24/06/2016

The God of Time

With an eclipse of love
My life you started with a beat
Like a knock on the door
To the world you had me freed
You painted me with your colours
Until I blossomed to your heat
But I did not know you or where you were
And no closer in my sleep
I now wake up
As time waits for us to meet

Placing me in her arms
You showed me how soft this heart can be
And how magnanimous yet tender
Walking amongst my father's feet
A gift limited yet limitless
Beginning with a seed
Ending with time, but time itself will
Wait for us to meet

No matter if roads never end
Until I have no feet
No matter if the path will never bend
Until all I can do is retreat
No matter if it's a bitter end

Burning tarmac off the street
The clocks will wait in the end
As time waits for us to meet

I weighed you with my mortal love
A scale my heart will balance
I measured you without mercury
With the heat inside my arteries
I loved you till the last draw of breath
I loved you both lungs deep
I loved you till the seconds ended
Until my final deed
I loved you till the grave
As time waits for us to meet

Taher Adel
01/07/2013

This Place Was Once Heaven

This place was once heaven
We used to cast our eyes upon each other
Knowing our hearts match in flow
Overflowing in innocence
Tides of joy pressing against the shore
But now I see deserts that were once valleys
Where life has all but gone
And all that is left of it is a space between a heart beat
Intermittently beautiful
There is a confusion in my mind
My thoughts were once an ocean
Pristine, full of life of every kind
Now full of death of deeds lost in time
Lost in hurt
Tasting the old salt of my tears
Wishing I can pause time
Mute screams
And live between the fragments of my dreams
Because at times it feels like it's more than I can bare
What happened to the childhood that we all used to share?
That is the cancer of my mind
Growing out of His absence
He showed me my childhood
And took it away
But left me with memories like freshly blown glass

Childhood smells of freshly cut grass
Smiles that once melted our parent's hearts
Happiness and contentment sourced from inside
A memory of the purity of our souls
The purity we eternally seek.

Taher Adel
02/10/2012

A Testimony

I was once a pearl growing between the
fingers of Your abundant care
Hiding beneath the crevices left by Your mercy
I abandoned my shell and now no longer own my beauty
The beauty You gave me
Giving up the tender kiss of the ocean
for the eyes of a greedy world
I now hide behind my thirsty tongue in a sleep of silence
Hiding my sins under pillows that dream them away
Seeking refuge from behind the walls of emptiness
as my hungry heart fails to bleed again.
Dying
My heart has become a glass ornament
in the hands of this careless world
In the world of heart breaks and high
cliffs it shatters into shards
That I cannot pick up without bleeding
I use the memories to clot the wounds
Because I am ashamed to seek Your
tender cure in this state of greed
I reminisce about the years
The years that I sought Your presence when
sadness took hold of me without realising
My tears themselves were created by
You to carry my anguish quietly

I sought Your nearness when the world had
abandoned me without realising each return
of breath Was Your reply to my calamity
I sought Your heeling as sins crippled me away from You,
not knowing each time I bled the scars that remained were
reminders of how many times You had truly healed me
From the surface of my heart to the surface of my skin
From the depth of my breaths that find home in my lungs
To the depth of my thoughts that quake in my mind
You created me such
A testimony of Your endless love.

Taher Adel
29/04/2012

Sustained

I write and I pollinate paper with my thoughts
Hoping to be held by their roots when
death frowns at my finished days
And time calls out no more
I call out to You
Knowing a question needs neither hook
nor bait to catch its answer
The same way you whispered life
Into my start
When I knew you not but as the light to my darkness
The existence to my nothingness
The continuance of my end
I surrender to my need for You
From my umbilical dependence
To the subconscious thought behind my final breath
I have tried to understand you through
the eyes that You have created
Only to bear witness to the proof of my creation

Each soul communicates to You
Through the strength that You have instilled into them
Amid the debris a child pushes back tears
Soon breaks because even mountains erode in time
But nobody sees the strength behind that silent wait
Nor sees how a mother has knitted her home

From a thousand silken webs of pain
And fed her children hope from a million broken hearts
What's more beautiful than a smile
suspended by a quenched heart?
Contentment sits in the heart just as water sits in a lake
Yet I drown my heart with the world when You have
Created for me a sustainable fountain

I write because it is the strength you have given me
So, I have scattered my being between my letters
Hoping they will find You blindly
I write because my mind hides a tragedy
A burdened cup, full and waiting to spill
The plot is death, tears provide the ink
until the heart stops writing
I yearn for You when my sighs collapse against my breath
But I need You most when my soul
collapses against my heart
I light a flame but will soon blow it away knowing
life is a candle placed on an empty throne
Gone but will it reclaim the kingdom
you have destined it for?
I write quenched by the favours that
choke me away from You
I write while being loved

Knowing your love for me is the pinnacle of guidance
While my love for You is the shadow of worship
It grows from within and crosses over to the other
Over an invisible bridge, to sit on the podium of the heart
But what podium am I sincerely worthy
of when I love You at my worst
Yet claim to end my letters faithfully?

Taher Adel
20/01/2010

Forever Destined

My heart wraps around His existence just
as my eyes wrap around the night sky
Taking in the beauty of the stars
My eyes now seek what's beyond the veil
The sentences behind the words
Letters forming suns and words universes
Sentences are a dozen words
Bundled within a heartbeat
Singing but the ears cannot hear
Just as the sun burns, little do we feel
But we grow to listen
What we fail to hear within
My ears are lullabied to rest by ancient tongues
Taught to move to His love
Tamed birds flying with the breath of angels
Lions made of paper, bravely folded upon heavenly creases
Ready to be dipped into the ink
Of His ocean
The pool of love that caresses the land
Teasing its hard interior
Providing comfort to its sharp edges
But asking for nothing in return
As the sky imitates its wonderful blue
Just as your shadow is imitating you

Forever chasing
Forever belonging
Forever destined

Taher Adel
24/12/2011

Writing Another Page

Locked in thought realising the cage that is my mind
Is all I really have right now
It carries me like the flame carrying the candle
Blown away by the slightest breath
Shortening as the days melt by
I find it grows stronger when I remember you
But it leaves me guilty that I seek
The heat of your flame only when I am weakened
Weakened by the cold whispers of the world
Whispering their darkness into every step I take
I find myself falling after each hurdle
Like the crispy leaves of yesterday
Falling into your lap like an eternal father
Only to grow again through your heat
But why do you extend a hand when
I have left you behind?
Like one of many memories
Stacked beneath the sins of my world
Only to blow away the dust when
there's nothing else to turn to
No doctor can stitch this wound of emptiness
Nor magician can cast it away
I know your presence is the only
thing that can fill the void
That eats my flame from inside

I've known it for a long time
But I am scared and the guilt is my curse
I would not rob from the rich
Yet here I am attempting to steal from You
Tricking you into loving me
Caring for me
As I decorate myself with the dirt of the world
And dance in the wild fires of mortality
I am not worthy of your love
Yet it has always completed me when
it has touched my soul
At times drowning me into thinking I do not need it
But here I am
Writing another page
Knowing I will end up writing books

Just begging you…

Taher Adel
06/09/2011

Heart

A piece of flesh
Given new
To play the drum
To the beat of life
Until childhood passes
And the notes are gone
And there it is
Weak and rough
Still and cold
Trying to remember
It's childhood song

Taher Adel
02/11/2017

It Is He

It is He who listens to our deepest fears
Listens to the sorrowful laments of our hearts
Like an infant in a cradle
Listening to it cry in its darkest nights
Listening to it sing in its brightest days
He feels the joy behind every smile
And the pain behind every tear
He's the caring eye
When no eye would settle upon ours
When we feel no love from the world
That built us up and brought us down to our knees
It is He who accepts our kneels when the world
Only accepts us on our feet
It is His remembrance that keeps my tides crashing
He's the home this traveller has always been searching for
When my sins left scars
Scars became maps
And these maps lead to Him
It is He who finds us beneath the tree
Looking for shade from the world
When memories plague our mind
Nightmares blur our daylight
And pain numbs our hearts
It is He who is the cure for our ailments
By prostrating, soul and mind

He is a wealth of a different kind
A wealth founded on love
He is the darkness that surrounds
The stars of hope
He is our stability
When the universe dances in our minds
He is the crescent that signals
Our beginning
He is the brightness that eclipses
The moon of our ending
He is the one that calms
The rhythmic flares of the sun
So that the world may feed
He is the reason the sun sinks
In the western sky
Only to rise again, for life
The light does not deny
Nor would He deny
Yet we, the nothingness, portraying arrogance
Underneath the planets and constellations
Cannot thank a little?

Taher Adel
03/09/2011

Do You Know Of That Candle?

Do you know of that candle?
That lights up this room
A room with two windows velvet black
Gazing at the world, as the world gazes back
With a skin thin door
And a tear or two at its shore
All lighten up by this candle
Yet this candle resides only in darkness
With a hand, unseen, as it's harness
A candle that burns furiously
Yet it tames its flames for us
To sizzle on the worlds exterior in all calmness
Out of sight, yet instilling warmness
As if the world is its egg
An egg that is just about to hatch
But it's no more than a candle lighten
by the flick of a match
A candle that melts at the corner of our rooms
Melting and rising as we but grow
Like that rose with our petals on show
Despite being anchored and held by thorns
Blushing in the sunshine, as beauty we adorn
Realising we are but gifts of God.

Taher Adel
22/10/2009

A Tale of the Sun and the Moon

I speak of a tale, a tale of the sun and the moon
And how they gently eclipsed that day at noon
I speak of the sun of hope, and the moon of salvation
I speak of the bright fire of mercy, the finest creation

A tale of how the Sun brought the Moon on display
Of how the moon was flaunted throughout that very day
When the fiery palms of the Sun
clenched the Moon's fingertips
There and then they fell into eclipse.

Taher Adel
2007

I Plead

Reflections of sunlight rays, once upon a day
I pondered if there was another sky
More serene and fair
Or if existed another sunshine
Which shines a different glare?
Maybe a moon that burns crimson red
Or a dancing sun instead?
As much as I endlessly reflected
No closer I became
My lord and I, so distant
So far, far away
I plead
Let my heart become your temple
Like the bloodstream I return
Let my soul become your sky
So your shelter I will earn
Let my words become a breeze
So I blow myself to you
Let me fall onto my lowly knees
In sincerity, I want it true
Let me cry honest tears
So your forgiveness I pursue
Let me rise like a tide
In remembrance during prayer
Let my love not subside

So your lordship I can declare
So let me, let me be your slave
Because nothing greater I can be
Nothing more one could crave
Because with you its eternity

Taher Adel
11/10/2008

Do I Love You Sire?

Do you remember each ant you crushed?
Each fly you squashed
Did they expect the unexpected?
I am no stronger if not weaker
Immortal I perceive myself
Yet the clock in my heart only counts down
And will stop at any digit
Life is a burning rope
A rope one cannot grip or hold
Death is often said to be life's mystery
But the mystery is life itself
At 18, I've already surpassed the expectancy of millions
Ropes cut short
Am I thankful? Never, Satan whispers
It may come in disguises, but death is one
In a world where temptations prevail
I question You about my unanswered wishes
But if it weren't for You, I would not exist
Yet I openly sin
Even as I write this I know
I will come back again tainted with sin
When I suffered I huddled your book
Which lay dormant as I basked carefree not long ago
Who do I think I'm fooling?
The only fool is I

I'll promise myself, but I'll soon let go
Satan's whispers would echo
For I have become a slave of desires
Fragile and hollow
Blown away by the sinning breeze
Like the dead autumn leaves
Which would return to bask in your glory
In there season and only there season
Why can I not become a rock?
A steadfast mountain
Life is an ocean
And we all swim its lengths
But with no arms I would always retreat
Now I dishonourably admit
I am the biggest hypocrite
So, do I love you sire
Or do I just fear the fire?

Taher Adel
06/08/2008

The Beauty Of He

As the heart of my heart opened wide
I thought of 'He'
Possessor of endless majesty
I pondered
At how many superlatives I could ascribe
Or how a pen could justly describe
His beauteous love
That stretches beyond this lifeless paper
The ink runs low
My eyelids tire
How can I describe you
O' Sire?
If the beauty of creation
Leaves me in wonder
Will the beauty of your lordship
Destroy me asunder?
In rapture my soul was hushed
Yet in his love was grazed and brushed
His enthroned loftiness
No words could reach
It remains beyond boundless sea
Of imagination that enthrals
You and me
Unlike the majestic orb of night
The glorious fire of day

And all life's beauty on display
His beauty is beyond the astonished eye
Leaving the chords of soul in sigh
The beauty of the ignited candle
Left me inarticulate
So the Sun, could I handle?
For that was the beauty of 'He'
Possessor of endless majesty

Taher Adel
11/09/2008

Soul

A secret breath
Inhaled
Like rain on soil
To come alive
To walk the earth
Until He calls it back
Exhaled

Taher Adel
24/11/2017

My Words Mean Nothing

My words mean nothing
Assembled words like assembled breaths
Like a brittle wind that leaves me exactly where I lay
But a brittle wind creates a mountain in a span of years
Like an idea planted through deaf ears
So let me seek you like the birds that
never fail to sing at sunrise
I found miracles in our dialogue before,
and words of poetry fail to describe
And lines of ink can only say much
Cleverly glossing over my arrogance and hypocrisy
But your mercy always looks beyond the gifts
I hold and the foolishness I display
And you see me not through human eyes of mud
and water but for the tarnished soul that I am
Begging to be cleansed once more
I asked for comfort yet comfort brought
me further away from you
And only extended away the dusty corner of my soul
I asked for all things beautiful yet I forgot
the beauty of the hand that granted it
I only saw you through the eyes of
pain and a stomach of hunger
I'm dependant until I'm independent,
and that's how it will always be

I cloud my radiant heart with arrogance,
I refuse love to those I judge don't deserve
it yet I've never deserved it myself
The more you planted yourself within me the
more I sought the weed of this world to destroy
the fruitful garden you've sown for me
Weed planted so deep that I foolishly water it
thinking it would one day become beautiful
But not everything beautiful leads to you,
yet you lead to everything beautiful
I live in a body which can't wait for the day it leaves me
Yet we still flaunt it to please eyes of
lust and hearts full of rust
Forgetting one day we'll be left with our grave stone's dust
But enough rhyming because my death
won't follow a lyrical pattern
Nor my grave a rhyming metre
Undeserving yet you give me gifts like poetry that I
can yield like an escalabar, wielded by my heart
Yet it's not only my heart you bring life to
In other hearts you instil love for me,
yet my love for you I distil?
You bestow me with souls who think of
me before themselves, yet I only think of
you when nobody thinks of me

I exist so long as I am remembered but there comes
a time when we're forgotten yet you never forget
You know more than anybody that I'm an open wound
I can either heal or get worse
Just like an open book
I can be a tale of success or loss
But my words mean nothing.

Taher Adel
18/08/2010

Sinless Childhood

Here you'll come to read
The bewildering tale of a simple seed
That started life in a world of fruit
Perfect from what he could see
Peace from what he could feel
His mind care-free

One day as he slept under the sun of gold
He fell from his mother's paw
Terrified, he tried to hold
Alas, lost, she was home no more
Nearby she remained and stood
But of no use, an old friend
She was his sinless childhood
There he lay, withered on the ground
Fed by the sun and the cloud that poured down
As time elapsed, he was growing
Stronger he slowly became
Not long, his leaves started showing
Now he was no longer the same
Arrived the voices, the blowing
His new friend, Satan the hurricane
The sinning breeze dragged his leaves along
The deceiving darkness, blinded him in dismay
Quenched, yet drowned by demon showers

Slaughtered, a powerless piece of wood
His branches tangled, from sins decay
For this was the result that followed childhood

He cried
Such a waste this short life of mine
No guidance in me within
From Satan's hand I chose to dine
The very filth that led to sin
He cried
Had I been patient in His godly power
And outstretched my roots within the ground
I would have surely become home to blooming flowers
That beautify heavens surround
Pondering, now I wish
If ever possible, if I ever could
I would like to return to childhood

Taher Adel
01/09/2008

Gently Pluck and Pull

The Book unfolds free
And from it words are gently sung
Like the pounding of the sea
Upon the crown of my tongue
Now drinking from its skies
Absorbing the mystic showers
Feeding my hidden treasures
As I stroll amongst the flowers

Sunlight rays comes forth to the heart of my humble home
Leaving their blazing sun
And upon my leaves they roam
A trail of its sweet fragrance
Inhaled in a set of words
Like a bee amidst a hive
Or a colourful flock of birds

My roots carefully implanted
In forever forgiving soil
Through that I am enchanted
As my bud gracefully uncoils
Fed by verses of flowing fountains
Words of endless power
And letters like moving mountains
All graced by I, the flower

Now pages like petals between my fingers
Gently pluck and pull
In the name of He, the most Gracious,
The most Merciful

Taher Adel
23/01/2009

Imperfect Man In An Imperfect World

Imperfect man in an imperfect world
Like a wound in the sky, a moon that is hurled
A fractured glow adorning the darkest of nights
Yet in day a silent sphere out of His sight
Horizons diminish as the moon manifests
Stars gather as man quietly rests
Winds sweep and whisper a gentle blow
As streams and rivers like mercury glow
The day enfolds and the night descends
For one day is done and closer becomes my end
I try to thank You for everything thus far
Even when life breaks open the chords of my soul
When sins disguise themselves flamboyantly
And Satan approaches in delirious elegance
Only to fool the fool that is I
I try to be thankful for it's the least I could be
Even when death rattles forth doubts in my mind
And I witness the corruption of myself and mankind
I try harder to be thankful when I reach my peak
As I am examined with what I perceive
to be the most arduous of trials
Till tears mutilate the immortal soul of mine
Leaving the heart to cry and mourn alone

Carrying the burden of this world in the smallest of rooms
Once bleeding joy now bleeding fear and regret
But I understand that these trials are a test of faith
For that reason my merciless soul tightens in shame
And my heart of stone breaths a rock hard sigh
For questioning the infinite wisdom of yours
When you took what you took and expected a reply
A reply overdue
An Imperfect man awakening from
his imperfect past and into
The present that will only bring forth
The future
A new start.

Taher Adel
09/2009

Nest of Hope

I am an embrace that can take your heart away
An answer to your broken wishes
Deep with truth, I can move the rigid world
No human eye can question how, what, or when
Because I am not a rhyme from any man's old pen
I am a song that not every soul can sing
Softer than heavens kiss upon an angel's wing
I can sing to you of virtues and what your heart holds dear
Of oracles and prophets and why you live in fear
When you stray from the path of life, I can light your way
Whispering sweet endearments that no other one can say
I am a riddle to those whose cannot see me
Whilst a tale of hope to those who see
I am the words that whisper in the darkest depths of night
Beneath the many masks you wear, I
still cross your sinning eyes
And be the goodness of soul or the
pain of your endless lies
I judge you through my letters and
teach you through my words
For I am a nest of hope sheltering you, my birds
I am new to every lens and not a product of the ages
As you find your world flicked through my many pages

But it is only when you choose to meet
my gaze, you'll finally know
How, what or when and only then, will you grow

Taher Adel
09/02/2009

Blind

What if God created you blind?
And we told you of all the amazing
structures and the colourful intricacies
That you cannot see
Would you believe them?
What if God created you deaf, and we painted a
picture showing you what it feels like to hear
All the wonderful sounds that surround us
Would you believe them?
What if God created you with no long-
term memories to fall back on?
And someone mentioned your childhood
Would you remember it?
What if God created you heartless
And we showed you how to love another
Would you still feel it?
What if God created you
With a barrier between you and Him
How would you go about finding Him?
God is found where money and possessions hold no value
Where there is no door, no wall or roof
Where he cannot be enclosed in a space
Nor constrained by size or shape
He cannot be painted in colours nor seen by eyes
He cannot be reduced and encrypted into a handset

Nor drawn or written with hieroglyphs or alphabets
The universe cannot contain Him, yet
you want our thoughts to?
Languages can only describe but not reveal
Because God can be grasped but not seized
Spoken of but not breathed
Loved but not perceived
His signs mimicked but not recreated
His miracles explored but not solved
Life can be traced but not drawn
He is found outside the confines of time and space
God is Great
Yet Great is only a word
God is Almighty
Yet by what scale can his might be weighed?

Taher Adel
18/03/2016

The Fallen

He started off as the closest in orbit
The biggest star in the perpetual rhythm of worship
Swimming through a sea of constellations
Orbiting the oneness
Until he was too grand
Too far and too bright
To see the flicker of pride
Light up a match to his wings
Until all that was left was darkness and ashes
And that's how he became known as the Fallen.

Now he is a blackhole
His core is dark where it was once light
A rogue son
A tainted nebula
All consuming
His arms are invisible
His whispers are silent yet penetrative
His darkness reels us in
Feasting on our desires
Pulling us into his universe
And out of ours
By weakening the gravitational pull of our childhood
The pure rope to the Oneness
Now we spiral down

No rope or safety net
The rogue sun drags us down and into
The nothingness
Where we hope to climb out
But all we find are deep craters of sins
Now we too are fallen…

Taher Adel
18/12/2017

The Power Of Man's Will

Son of Adam sin he craves
While the sea seeks not of thrill
Yet momentum gave it waves
Like the power of man's will

O' Lord,
I wish I could control my desires, all my hopes and whims
And direct my prostration to you
from all my heart and limbs

No boat has ever wished to sink
Yet here we are wet and drenched
Collapsing, breathless and on the brink
But I thought sin would quench?

O' Lord,
I wish I could guide my sails and float into your path
Sometimes this earthly flesh dear
Lord only heeds your wrath

Simply routine
Sin is taken so shamelessly in our stride
We grow it vast, and plough it clean
And re-grow and plough again in pride

O' Lord,
I wish I could grow your love and harvest it with care
But at times this earthly flesh dear
Lord simply cannot bare

The tongue allures with the softest of words
Yet that same tongue sternly berates
A falcon one day, a dove another
Hypocrisy, our soul it desecrates

O' Lord,
I wish I could control this tongue
and the things it has to say
Sometimes this earthly flesh dear
Lord so much gets in the way

Who deserves a thousand burns from the sun?
Because the devil has written his fate
A fate in which he cannot run
Only to suffocate

O' Lord,
I wish I could rewrite my life and all the things I've done
Every word I've murmured, every sentence I've begun

One still seeks comfort from what's between
The book, wisdom that exudes from its walls
Untouched, lost, forgotten and unseen
Words that amaze, mesmerise and enthral

O' Lord,
I wish I could take in your book and cover it with my soul
Sometimes this earthly flesh dear Lord loses all control

In that darkness one awakens
To see a tiny ray of light
A warmth of glow that beckons
And dispels away the night

O'Lord,
I wish I could not stray away from
your boundless gracious love
Sometimes this earthly flesh dear
Lord thinks he's got enough

Son of Adam's sin lead him to the grave
While the sea went back to still
He became his own man's slave
Through the power of man's will.

O' Lord,
I wish if I see another morning, another chance you'd give
To help me shed this human flesh, and for You only I live

Taher Adel
12/06/2009

Walking Where I Shouldn't Be

I find myself lost, so lost I cannot see
Walking blindly in a world, walking where I shouldn't be
Through darkness, where a light was once meant to shine
Like a guiding star, from a world that was never mine

I wake in the morning knowing, my death is surely near
I get up on my feet, and take in His for granted air
Feeling guilt in my heart, lost in its defying sea
As I top my mountain peak, as my sins wander free

I stare into the eyes, of those who are close and dear
But still when darkness visits, closer becomes my fear
Fragments of once good, now seem to float away
The only thing I yearn for, is the hope of a brighter day

Maybe one day, my repentance will be true
And the sky that I once loved, will return to its blue
But it's too late, here ends life, what we used to share
As I look across the room, to see death over there

As my remains are taken beneath this lonely ground
My soul, can you forgive me for letting you down?
You kept with me, treasured from the time of my birth
I'm sorry for destroying you, on this very earth

People mentioned my presence, 'will always be felt'
So now I leave them, leaving their eyes to lightly melt
As they circle my body, as it's all they have of my being
The person they once loved, that
they will no longer be seeing

The body of torture I leave, here in your care
As I embark in another, one I'm assured I shall not bare
Now I wish I wasn't so lost, and everything I had seen
Walking in his world, walking where I should have been

Taher Adel
27/11/2008

Filter

If you could see with my eyes, and filter
the world through my lashes
You'll see how the light precedes the
dark, how fire becomes but ashes
How the moon is but a soft white glow,
a reflection of a burning light
You'd wonder how you lived so long,
with that same blanket at night.

If you could hear what I hear filtered
through the vibrations of my bones
Ignoring the sounds that loiter on the
tongue and life's repetitive tones
You'll hear the sounds of creation and
the murmurs of our existence
And you'll wonder why your ears couldn't
hear through the distance.

If you could feel what I feel filtered through
the folded creases of my finger
Placing your heart between those palms,
upon the scars, let them linger

You'll see your soul intertwine and manifest
within each beat of your being
Now you wonder how, why and what you're not seeing?

Taher Adel
26/02/2010

Go On

Go on, climb the clouds if you dare
Take the world and all its riches, dear
Reach the heights you loved, but beware
That this world is but a turning sphere
And your cloud will not stay still, so fear
From becoming that storm bellowing everywhere
Indeed
Your inner darkness will search very far and very near
To find and embrace your one and only fear
The loss of this and that and all you hold so dear
Till you yourself shall wield that devils spear
Now former sins seem very small and very mere
Why?
Because you sold yourself to the world, my dear

Taher Adel
23/03/2009

In Doses

This is me; here I stand, on the highest peaks of despair
Gazing across my land of sin, as the
clouds, now shed my tear
I took the poison, in growing doses,
till it took away my sight
The glistening gems that reflect His
love, the gems of mortal light
My eyes now hide, like pearls,
between the craters left by sin
As the lids drop down, like thunderbolts,
and lock them deep within
Trails of once an honest tear, still
trace down this lonely cheek
The trail that began with light, now ends in destined bleak

With no sight, I wander, fail, and
ponder, so close yet so aimlessly
Looking, searching, to no avail, and
yet I continue endlessly
So the doses increase, slither up,
and across my desert route
Locking thoughts in their tracks,
ending my mind's pursuit
Clouding the light, the rays that shine,
from the beauty of curiosity

Casting shadows, holding hostage, my minds luminosity
Starving what life remains inside, the
start, the end, the minds decay
Till the leaves of the mind, with the arms
of the breeze, just simply fly away

The poison skipped the soft and moistened
tongue, instead leapt for the heart
Because the tongue, was an evil of
its own, already torn apart
Like any tool of Satan, it could be as
sweet as the nectar of the bees
So sweet, it could bring down a king
and his kingdom to its knees
Unlike the tongue, the heart was one with
his word, a simple yet peaceful land
Built for love, made from love, carried
by love, for that it was so grand
As soon as the poison bypassed its doors,
and opened the love filled barriers
Erasing lessons etched upon this naive yet
honest organ, destroying its interior

Now swaying with the world, another sheep
from the herd, in the current of the stream
So thoughtless, so blind and soulless, I
fail to even fly a simple dream
Even with the sun out to play, prey kept
away and my wings spread open wide
The wind, the whole blue sky and
its puffy clouds by my side
As if my dream, hung ripe as a peach,
a diamond of a glistening star
Close, very close, though it seems it was
simply shining, shining too far
Because to the blind of the world, I
sacrificed my one and only sight
To the ill of this world, the deceitful,
I sold my mind, my light
To the numb and heartless, I surrendered
the flowing rivers of my heart

To Satan I simply sold my life.

Taher Adel
12/09/2009

Surface of Her Heart

I see my past in her ageing eyes
I see my once upon a times
I see my fears through her tears
And my lived happily ever after smiles

I see myself fly beyond the realms of kings
I see myself grow out of her shadowed wings
I see my heart soften from stone to sand
And realise hers must have been so grand

I remember as she shone through my eyes
I remember how time fled and stars could not improvise
I remember pain trembled on her wisp of touch
And books could not write about mother's love this much

I remember her nearness as death takes its steps
I remember her as pain expands like cobbled webs
I remember floating on the surface of paradise
And here I am
Forever sleeping on the surface of her heart

Taher Adel
22/09/2011

Angels Whisper

Angels whisper to one another
About the finest angel, my mother
Through her eyes I witnessed the glimmer of the moon
And basked in her sun from dawn to noon
My world was moulded by her very hands
Just as the farmer would plough his lands
Under her wing I found my home
In her love I endlessly roam
I blossomed in her pure reflection
And unfolded through her affection
An equal to her there cannot be
She is the mother He gave to me

'Heaven Lies Under The Feet Of The Mother'
Not entirely true
I see heaven in her tender eyes
I see the seventh of the skies
I feel it under her gentle touch
I hold it when our hands do clutch
I smell it in her scented clothes
Like a bee amidst a blossomed rose
If I could have chosen, I would have picked no other
To be my friend, to be the angel that is my mother

Taher Adel
4/12/2008

Mothers Love

Mothers love? An unidentifiable fusion
Often it is the centre of confusion
Mistaken for an insignificant allusion
Just look at her eyes, serene, alive
Upon those glares my soul will thrive
Through those stars my pulse shall drive
She kept me throughout the years
Away from the dark and gloomy fears
Under the umbrella of her gentle tears
She dressed me with life's attire
Shielded me from the living fire
When it should have consumed me entire
Mothers love is something you cannot devour
Take away, destroy nor empower
It is like the fragrance of a flower
Separated they cannot be
A lock without a key
My mother and me

Taher Adel
17/06/2008

Love

An ocean that spills
From heart to heart
Like ink from page to page
A language
Spoken from eye to eye
Like the walk between two hills

Taher Adel
09/09/2017

Tearful Effigy

Memories are beautiful until all you have left are memories
Faces that you'll never see again
A seed that will never grow the same
Old smiles that you cannot reciprocate
Love that is now a hurricane
Yet they still linger with every common smell
Reappearing underneath every lifted shell
And before you know it, you're drowning in their spell
Drowning in a pool of precious fragile memories
With every tear, you slowly become a tearful effigy
While their body rests six feet below, hidden deep
Time will pass and tears will dry
But the torture plays on in memories.

Taher Adel
31/05/2017

The Heir

Time is broken, but the clocks keep churning
The light is forgotten, and the world is burning
Men seek darkness, and the good is turning
Until there is no hope left except you returning

The gate finally opens and the false king abdicates
The clock strikes twelve, just like prophecy narrates
The sun turns its face, the earth to your light dilates
The Heir is here, but will our souls to yours congregate?

Taher Adel
09/07/2017

Time Lord

They call him the Redeemer
The Saviour
The Successor
The final breath of life
The Maschiach, the Messiah
The Lord of the Age
The Liege of Time
The Sovereign of Justice
The Inheritor
The Son of Mercy
The Heir to the Sword
An artist who paints in shades of peace
A poet whose words are strikes of justice
A man who travelled time till time declared him Lord.

Taher Adel
07/03/2017

The Four Seasons of Déjà Vu

I was a newly blossomed
The wind played rings around my petals
Angels visited me occasionally
As a peaceful slumbering child
Until I was awoken from my slumber
By the whispering sonnets of mother earth
Teasing my roots into growth

Fully bloomed
Under the exhausted sun of summer day
I bore fruits to signify my sweetness
Arrogantly basking in the august horizon
Dancing to the rare monsoon of rain
I was full of strength
As faceted eyes of whirling colour reflected in my green

But soon my leaves began to age
Longing for more breath while my roots lusted for death
The wind vibrated against me, singing an apology
An apology to each leaf that dived to the
ground from my many branches
Twirling in the wind like they've done this
A million times over
Knowing death was not new to them

Now the trees oscillate
The wind croons to the chorus of winter's nip
I was an emancipated man chained by dreams
Now a chained man scared to wish his time away
Afraid I'll never wake up again
Like a blizzard, sins have turned me brittle
Writing over the cracks only breaks me more
Wishing I could write beneath the dark sky
So I am not swayed away by my previous pages
But the darkness has blackened my heart away
The cold has left its softness frost bitten
The candle of my youth blown away
By the howling wind, as my branches wane
Through each tear I sift I am matched by a droplet of rain
Now mother earth buries me in her arms
To be a lesson
A lesson for you
A lesson taken from the four seasons of
Déjà vu

Taher Adel
30/01/2012

Candle beauty

They told me I was too ugly, too different
I was a sore to the eye, ruining the skyline
My people were beautiful and diverse
But I was told my job was to hide them
And so I did the best I can
But now I was ageing, my wrinkles spreading
No longer streamlined, and too cheap to be antique
So they convinced me to get surgery
This was public funding, my options were limited
My weakened organs ignored
They concentrated only on my body
Plastic surgery
They wanted me to look beautiful
They called it cladding
But what about the people we're trapping?
I was told to camouflage and just hide my belongings
But it was only a matter of time
If you place wax near a flame
It would always start melting
My people tried to save me
But my new face would just continue burning
In fear I tried to embrace them
Until all sides of me were igniting
My people trapped
And my smoke was squeezing

Them until their last choking breath
Voices screaming till the silence of death
The others wanted me to be beautiful
Here I am in the depth of night
Burning like a candle
Overlooking their quiet houses
Is this the beauty you wanted?

Taher Adel
24/06/2017

A reminder

A reminder to one's self, do not fret when
The feeling of vulnerability and weakness overtakes you
For it is a reminder for your souls to seek strength
But strength is only found in stability
And stability is only found in balance
And true balance must be everlasting
And very few things last beyond time
So do not seek the light of the fire
Rather seek the spark that lit it
Do not find comfort in a world designed to be fleeting
Instead shroud yourself in the warmth of He who build it
Let yourself witness His work in all that surrounds us
In beauty and even in things your eyes deem unsightly
As imperfection is testimony to that which is perfect
An equation that confirms the solution
So live your life seeking answers in doors that are open
And do not let your pride close doors behind you.

Taher Adel
04/01/2017

Final Promises

The moon witnesses another hide away
As the biting wind caresses
The soil of his new home
His mother sings the song of the broken
Singing endlessly till the broken heart cannot feel
Whispering final promises
Promises he can no longer keep
While our tarnished souls gather to bleed
Bleeding endlessly to his memory
Yesterday we lived sins unnoticed
Under hurrying feet
Seeing that burial soil mirror his once night sky
Seeing us through the soil
His only visiting stars
Stars that won't return every night
His voice never to be heard again
A tongue tied by the knot of eternal silence
His eyes never to be seen again
Blindfolded by eternal sleep
Living on in crushed memories
Reflected in the past
No time for building sandcastles
The end is here at last

Taher Adel
16/12/2011

Drowning

Weaving each second into
Something worthwhile
Piling each breath
Above another
While she watches me in denial
Drowning in an ocean of bed sheets
Like a dolphin
Diving
Into a world I haven't seen
Then back to mine
Back to her earthly face
My eyes wanting to say a thousand words
And her tears wanting a thousand more
Eyes slipping away
But my heart continues to stampede
Across the roman road of my lungs
Holding on to every last bit of this world
Holding on to her tears
Because the rest of the world isn't worth it
Why wouldn't my smile let her go?
I drown in her tears smiling
Drowning into a world
Where I can see the hidden waves
Behind every flap of a robin's wings
Like every thought lifted with each flap of my lash

Taking me into a world
A world that never dies
A world of poetry
A world so sublime
I write my name across
Every empty wall in my beloved's heart
I engrave my ink across it
As I listen to it sing
Singing to my memory

Taher Adel
16/05/2011

Death's Last Embrace

A lively son
Full of life
As his mother awaits him
I find him asleep on shards of suspended glass
I lift him from under the freezing night
And fly him back on the wings of the wind
Carrying his light soul back to the woman who bore him
Leaving his soul on the sill
She stares upon the window glass wishing
his shadow would reappear
Silent rain taps upon the window
As her heart breaks with the chirps of birds
Her world has slipped while the sun has risen
But there is no rainbow to pave the way

Onto the next soul
An aging woman
With injections numbing the pain
Just like the needles she once used with thread
When she sewed so tenderly
With the love she carried
In her hands, worn and weathered
Into colourful sheets and priceless garments
Knitting for new-borns as they grew into her smile
Now looking down

Into an empty room
With the only guest being myself as
I take away what she hoped
Others would treasure

Onto the next soul
A beautiful young woman
Wishing to be forever young and boisterous
Dressed up for one last twirl
With pretty pearls around her neck
Just below where her killers hands
Locked away her last breaths
Her eyes were wide and full
When I detached her soul with a
Kiss, gentler
Than life could ever
Offer
A woman of this world no more
As they laid her down
In silent contemplation
Death to beauty
But not a beautiful death
Enclosed in wood like an artefact
Not to be touched nor seen again

I know no name
Nor age
But they sleep, as they all do, in my arms
With a dream just beginning

Taher Adel
27/06/2011

Fleeting moments

Fleeting moments, that's all we have
Some we remember, others we forget
Some moments we share with people
And others we keep to ourselves
But all these moments are fleeting
And the pace of it all is overwhelming
Until we become just a timeline of moments
And the earth becomes just a huge camera
That captures our image throughout time
Some of us are remembered
As beauty that once touched the earth
Fleeting photo negatives
The more we remember them
The more colour can come through
But others are lost in it all
People that are short-lived
Shadows that pass through as just
Fleeting moments.

Taher Adel
30/02/2017

I Cannot Go To Sleep

As the final breath calmly breaks from my soul
I enter a valley where
Petals calmly break from delicate flowers
Under a wondrous moon of peace
Floating away in a place where days are but ease
Birthing sonnets with every sigh
To the sublime peaks of bliss I climb
On the wings of youth on either side
My mind drifts through splendid seas of certainty
As my soul crashes into intricate waves of calm
I'm in a garden filled with sparkling realities
No wrinkles across my face, no painful arm
The sun following my shadow like a breeze
Voices of children I follow on the hills
Love in my heart and spare it spills
I cannot go to sleep
I want to play till the morning appears in the skies
My heart is at rest within my chest
Leave it be

I breathe again
And here I am snatched away from where I've always been
Into forlorn roads and endless tunnels
Where love is but a chain and words but riddles

Until I wake up
Wake up to my childhood. My eternal childhood.

Taher Adel
05/04/2011

Written By You

Time is so vast yet swiftly moves
You cannot tinker with it as it is the script of life
That plays upon the stage
Of this murky sphere
Accompanied by the liveliest of audiences
That we call humanity
Yet it is we who write it
Before the Hand above

Every move you take moulds itself upon the stage
Followed by eager eyes
But tell me, how artistic are you?
Does the script control you?
Or do you orchestrate the script?
Tell me, what's the plot of your tale?
Do you act out a tragedy?
Or are you a king in fantasy?
Or perhaps even a jester of love
Bringing forth joy to the world, your audience

How confident do you move on stage?
How many risks will you take?
Moving through your scenes
Following what is written
But then you falter

And that alters the script
But not to worry, as the show must go on!

Quickly does the play reach its end
And there you are a character in conclusion
But you've just begun
You cannot start over
As the stage is booked only once
You could have done better?
Maybe, but the judgement has been made

Now time comes to take a bow
As the curtains draw to a close
Bouquets are thrown
Like soil upon a grave
A character once known
Now forgotten
In a once life-filled play
Written only
By you.

Taher Adel
3/12/2009

Once Upon A Time, I died

Once Upon A Time, I died
But just before that I began
To see the world in its true colours
Ocean blue and wild green
Were just shades of black upon a cloudy screen
I saw behind those innocent faces
The people we once knew as angels of this world
Were actually the devil in disguise
X was never that fragile daisy
Neither was Y that red flushed rose
Wilted flowers camouflaged
Each person lived a riddled tale
Inscribed upon the iris of their eyes
Full of dark and nervy secrets
Held by a belief that no one will realise
Writing this, I am in no way an exemption
For my tale may just begin
To riddle away in destroying me
Sin by sin
Because the path of corruption
Starts with a fountain of innocence
Which overflows till it drowns you over
Most often, there is no escape
Till the grave

But the grave is a tale just begun
Starting with 'Once upon a time, I died'

Taher Adel
10/09/2008

Festival of Stars

Away from the dwelling place of men
Under a festival of stars where the light of night hovers
But darkness still eats away to the sigh of the wind
In a location known only to my mind
He found me asleep against my own ignorance
Coiled in loose folds of shame
An orphan in a world that had abandoned me
Where worldly hope burnt men
Until they were lost in the white heat waves
Shadeless and helpless
Amongst the carcasses of broken and abandoned souls
Alone in the dying breast of the world
Just like the distant stars, this heart maybe beating
But it has been dead for a while
And its next beats would take it into dusk
With time gnawing against the walls
Unzipping it from a soul so eager
So eager to separate, hopeless
But he found me as if he knew
He knew I would be waiting at the guillotine of time
Like a mortal Jonah
Waiting to see the timeless patience in his eyes
And chase hope that has declared him a master
With a hand reaching back to me

He showed me how his scent made a
garden out of God's desert
An oasis out of the emptiness
Breathing life into my worldly death like Jesus
In a desert void of hope
His presence was Noah's ark
Turning sand into a rippling current of sea
The sea of me
Splitting me from my past, Moses
Building me like the walls of worship
Abraham
Until I was strong enough to walk
And follow the crunching sound of his feet
Into the mystified distance
Until the horizon was one with his light
Too bright
My fevered eyes locked on his shadow
Chasing him through clouds that rise and disappear
Running down the passage of time
Seeing nothing but him carrying me
Beyond contradiction
Like the holy book
Finally arriving where my ego can sink into the shore
Sinking into worship despite knowing
my strength knows no bound

Ali
Finally lifting my head from this dream
Looking up to see him fade into the distance
just as wind fades, Mahdi

Taher Adel
17/08/2012

Dear Awaited,

If I knew why I write
I probably would not be writing to you
I write not because I want to
I write not because I have to
I write because I'm taken back by your reality
I write to empty the tears in my pen
I write because I could not write before
Until that day
When you took a step followed by another
Into my home
Upon ebullient breaths of dawn
You greeted my pen one morn
I write because it's seen your soul
And it's tripped over its lines
And fallen
Into and unto its pages
Pages only my heart can read
As my pen sits upon its podium
Writing away
With the flow of ink
Steady and thick
A little twist and turn here
Into letters forming what I think
Reflected in these letters is a portrait
Underneath the paint a tangle of confusion

Hope and fear
As if I've birthed a thousand stars
Yet darkness surrounds me everywhere
I offer you my self portrait
So you may consider my soul
Knowing I can only reach you through words
Knowing you are reading this somewhere
So what if
What if you were a boat sailing into my imagination
Sailing so deep you collided with the rocks of reality
What if the figments of my imagination
are shadows of what's real?
As my mind sits under my heart's tree
Venting thoughts by building cities out of mist
And palaces on the sea
Weaving words into gaps once left by reality
What if the Mahdi appears in us?
Standing against the wall of our hearts
Before he appears against that cubic wall
What if the second coming is the return
of the light we were born with?
Unshackling our souls so we may help unshackle the world
I begin to float on the breeze of understanding
Knowing with every heartbeat there's
an echo of your footsteps

Down the hallway of time
But here I am, still broken
Falling between these cracks hiding
Flying dreams from land to land
In-between where mountains stand
With words offering my hand
To be taken away with you...

Taher Adel
24/05/2011

Weaving Seconds

Patiently waiting, dead set eyes and
anticipating that final sun rise
Yet here I weave each second by second into years but why?
Because I find his signs written in me before books
Signs of a promise that was once made
A promise of a Mahdi, A Mashiach, a final Messiah
Signs will follow suit from the verses of
Isaiah to the pages of Jeremiah
The earth grows cold and the skies turn
grey and their goes past another day
Yet here I weave each second by second into years but why?
Because I feel his presence growing between
the thorns giving life in a bloom
His presence is like an ever orbiting moon
Martyrs have had their wings clipped before they could fly
Just so he could appear like a crescent in a bright day's sky
Oceans flow and winds come by yet nothing
is breathed between you and I
Yet here I weave each second by second into years but why?
Because I was born to serve before I was born to live
Serving at the doorway of hope, with all my heart to give
Just like the sun throwing its light upon the skies
I gift these arms and every blink of my eyes.

Taher Adel
2010

Obscure as a hidden star

A tale of how a bud became a flower
Previously concealed within a gulf of space
A halo of anonymous power
Hidden between innumerable days

A life written only in story
Justice he shall emit
He will beam his solar glory
But a myth they called it

Numbers shall count his tallies
His signs shall be fulfilled
Seas will turn into valleys
And his people shall be killed

Forbearance like mould
Shall gather along the centuries
Another sign foretold
Another fulfilment he will please

He shall travel near and far
As his companions ripen well
Obscure as a hidden star
He awaits the holy bell

He is the expected deliverer
His appearance shall be a trial
Pure hearts will beat his harbinger
And the sunset shall gleam his smile

Taher Adel
2011

A Glimpse of him

In desperation I search, look and seek
His location through my heart that leaks
Each time the graceful birds are flying
My heart and soul unite in sighing
Every night as the moon peers down
And the sky adorns its twilight gown
I look between the hazy stars
And through shadows they disbar
For a glimpse of him, he who waits
Under moonlit nights for destined fate
But every night I fail in my pursuit
As the devil plays my sinful flute
I begin to find home in sinful temptations
And see the world through aberrations
Even as the sun beamed on wild green
Misted light pervaded the scene
Blind to beauty I became
Hopeless, a dire sense of shame
His existence I ignored and swayed
The great descendant I betrayed
The truth was that it did not really matter
What the eyes did see even if it did but flatter
For it is a painting of what the heart does utter
And my heart now knowing this can flutter
For I have seen the Mahdi's light

And it rises beyond this mortal sphere
To join lights with the hearts he holds dear
So, tonight as moonbeams shine at me below
I can finally look upwards for my
heart would equally aglow

Taher Adel
2007

Taming My Demon

My demon has always been a wandering beast
A beast that I let grow without a leash
His roars disturb my inner peace
And now it not only hunts, but eats and breeds
There is no beauty left in this beast
Just ugliness and venom dripping teeth
No remorse, no guilt, no retreat
This beast wants it all, without defeat
My demon has always been a wandering beast
But now it's time I finally tie a leash

Taher Adel
10/07/2017

Power of Time

When one sinks to doom from prime
Why does he blame the ruthless power of time?
Time, is the most precious item man possesses
Through it centuries followed each other
Through it we saw joy
And through it we suffered bitterness
As it goes swiftly by
Each individual said goodbye
To the world and all its fading sweet
What is done now shall not repeat
So do not add up your living years
For time can strike like the spears
And when it does
It is lost in no 'time' at all
For destined is your awaited call
Yet His love for me and you is timeless
Yet in his love we cannot devour simple time
It is only when time itself for you becomes a slave
When your heart throbs no more
As you succumb to the pressure of the grave
It is then and only then
That your tongue will taste the sweet of timeless
Eternity
Now let us measure time like the birds
Those that never fail to sing at dawn

Do not be the ones whose wings are wet
So split the days and carve the hours
So that time is in your control
Like a stream that through you flows
Time is divided into misguiding seasons
So let your seasons revolve around him
Seasons that you can pluck like flowers
Every day, not only in spring
The flight of time will then subside
From swift to slow
Now one can remain in eternal prime
For he has befriended the great power of time

Taher Adel
27/8/2014

State of Emergency

BREAKING NEWS
There is a state of emergency
Martial Law is now in effect
Your heart should remain indoors
Sympathy has been evacuated
And your tears quarantined
You will now hate, love, laugh, cry and smile
Only when your screen adjusts its pixels accordingly
To our new safety criteria's
To ensure your safety and freedom

BREAKING NEWS
There is a state of emergency
The Richter scale reads 7.86
The tectonic plates of your brain are moving too violently
You are thinking
You know
You command your heart to feel again
We are sending in a rescue mission
Operation: Sectarianism
Hang tight
We will save you from this tsunami of emotion

WARNING
Your computer has been infected
Somebody you know has infiltrated your hard drive
You must remove them from your "trusted website" list
Www.Your-Religion.com
Stay indoors while we erase your internet history
And be afraid otherwise we have no
option but to quarantine you too
Raise your firewalls with our pre-designated algorithms
Don't fear
Install M-alware Software
Muslim-Aware

BREAKING NEWS
We are now in a REAL state of Emergency
Our defences have been breached
A man has recognised his brother...

Taher Adel
24/06/2013

Worldly Imitation

I have dressed you up in bright rays of light
Made the earth grow from under your fiery palms
Just so that I could remind the world of him
Majestic I made him stand
Flaunting greatness capped in flames of beauty
Standing still, twelve planets aligned upon his orbit
No evil can touch the surface
Spearheading into peaking open endlessness
As his soul touched my throne's endless greatness
He was created
And perfection was a template taken from his creation
For surely you are but a burning copy
A worldly imitation
Just as I have sown your light into each plant
I have sown his name into the delicate heart of each child
This mercy will leave a path behind
For he is my mercy to mankind
I have built sculptures upon the silk of his heart
Placed words upon his mind like
Glaciers into flowing rivers of crisp crystal worth
Offering life, rebirth
To each listener, reader from the words he uttered forth
Civilisation will come and go
But just like you he would outlast them all
No empire can break his walls

For I have placed his name between the
chords of the soul and the heart
Like a secret buried between two floating mountains
Understand that I have created you
As a light in the midst of darkness
But you are but a portrait of his perfected beauty
As he holds beauty itself by its harness

Taher Adel
09/02/2012

Voices

Enter this child's mind through the
gate of his broken smile
Stroll through the garden of innocence which
now homes the graves of the loved
Death has quietened all voices that were once loud in play
But has left him with a few whispers
that he cannot take away

Voices once hoping to see tomorrow
in all its beauty, cold and new
Sun rising on dusky mornings silhouetting
through clouds full of blue
"We had hoped you had died with us in our
cube of happiness" they would say
Under the four walls made of joy, voices loud in play
Voices he cannot take away

He gazes at the castle of his childhood that
he had built from golden memories
Hiding in the many rooms that fade away with the years
Tears tracing prayers on his mind
Wishing tomorrow he'll finally open his eyes and breathe
And speak
Speak to the voices he cannot take away

How those small fingers were digging beneath the rubble
Looking for faces that once were and hands once warm
The depth of his love can only be realised
through an excavation of love
And he has been digging for what's long gone enough
A sorrow so short
That tomorrow none would know, and none would hear
The voices he cannot take away

Taher Adel
14/09/2012

More

You sent me letters one morning
Flown to me upon beautifully floated objects
that found themselves to my home
"Dear Child" you said
As your words fell upon my family
And the sentences collapsed my heart into rubble
Enough rubble for me to roam
You dropped phosphorous like poetry
Swapping metaphors of freedom with never ending walls
Tying death ribbons like full stops around
my sunshine till it was no more
No more.

For warmth you wrote that I should burn like black coal
Burn because my flesh was never meant for a soul
Burn until the pastel blue sky darkens
Until darkness surrounds me whole
For light you promised fireworks to end my day on a high
Promising me my last memory would be lights in the sky
But before dawn blinked I was
nothing but limbs upon ashes
No lights anymore
No more.

You may have been close, but you
still flew your words to me
Taking time to empty your ammo
in forms of painful poetry
I'm writing back because that's what pen-pals do
But instead I've chosen to walk my letters
Straight into your consciousness
The same way yours tore my life in two
Your sentences touched me deeply
In all meanings of the word
But I couldn't help but think
Of how much you loved your country
For you to do what you've done
How much you loved your country
But how much it belonged to me more

Taher Adel
01/09/2012

One Year On

One year on
I've lost count of the sighs that have
floated on the winds of despair
Lost count of each worried heart beat
from a mother in moments of fear
Lost count of each escaped breath from a choking child
Lost count of each eye turned blind
And each blind eye turned away from our plight

One year on
I've cried for your nocturnal nights of pain
And dreamt your slain away
But each morning dragged my fantasy to its knees
On a newly sharpened guillotine
You're still shackled they tell me
The vultures have not gone away
They've demolished places of worship
The graveyard is the only place you pray
Burying by day and hoping by night
That tomorrow will not take another away

One year on
I still see a tint of hope mounted on
the shrouds that fade away
Burying our pains deep below the ground

Because no eye wants to look this way
One year on
I see the smiles of a future birthed from
behind the resistant walls of yesterday
And see the precision of God's hand
Manifest on the delicate smiles
That head his way
One year on
And my people have become stronger
than the spine of freedom itself
Shouting but nobody listens
Death has become the language forced upon us
So all we can do is write
One year on

Taher Adel
17/03/2012

Love At First Plight

We met in a crowded place
Lost souls in a sea of names
You followed me from my lonely
Lamp lit street of dreams
To a pearl that caught my eye midstream
Thousands of golden candles burnt that night
Their fading wax for hope of light
I sang with the defiant flames
Shooting sparks through the dark
Bouncing off our tears
As you set our captured rainbows free
A million eyes saw us dance that night
And flow through time so fleetingly
A million eyes saw me hold you tight
As I sought your soul for answers to set me free
But dreams are lonely places
Yet you were adamant to breathe brazen hope into me
I've knitted my home from a thousand silken webs of pain
With each link I've paved my path ahead
Sculptured by the art of hope
All in your very name

You were freedom and I was plight
We were love at the first blink of sight

Taher Adel
14/02/2012

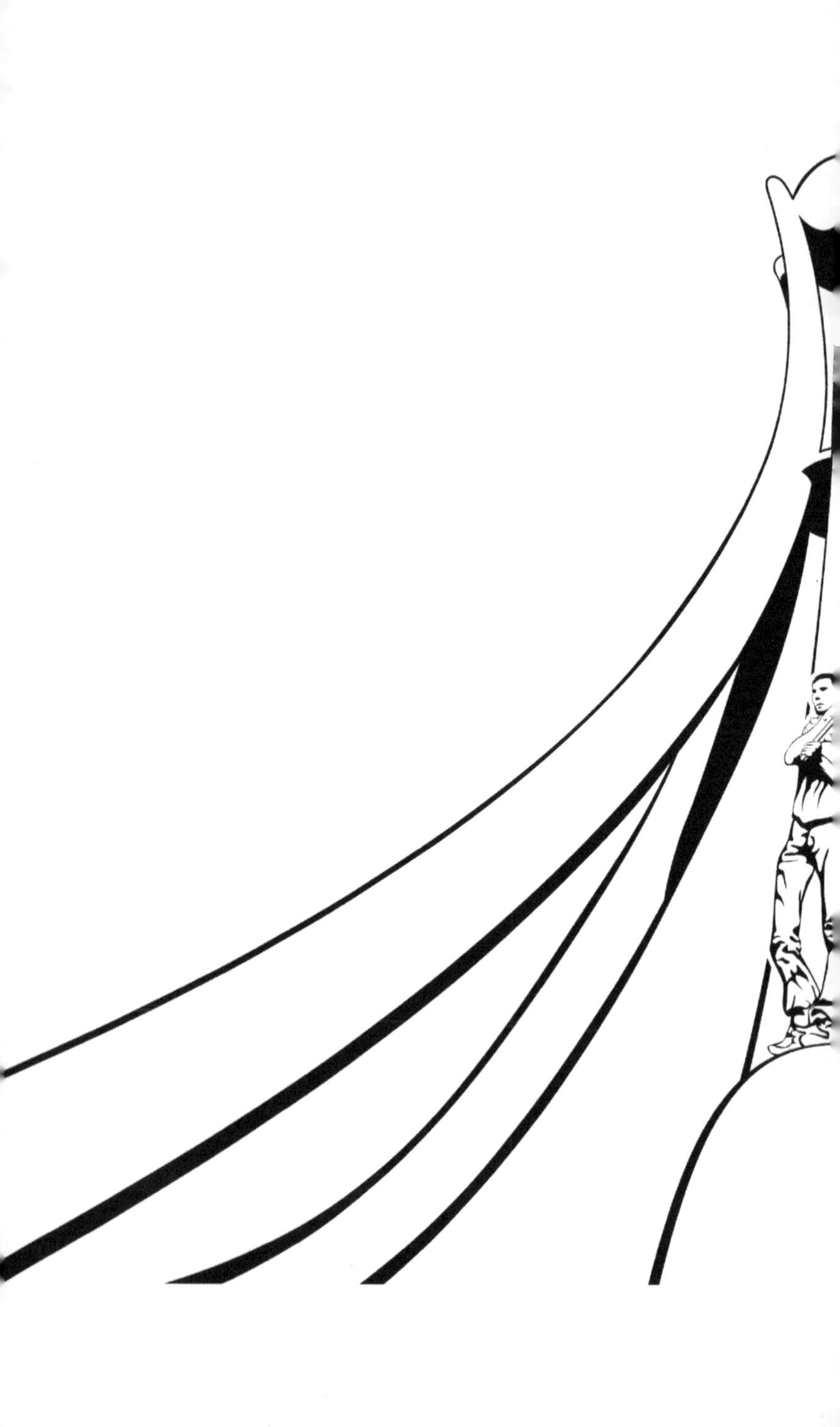

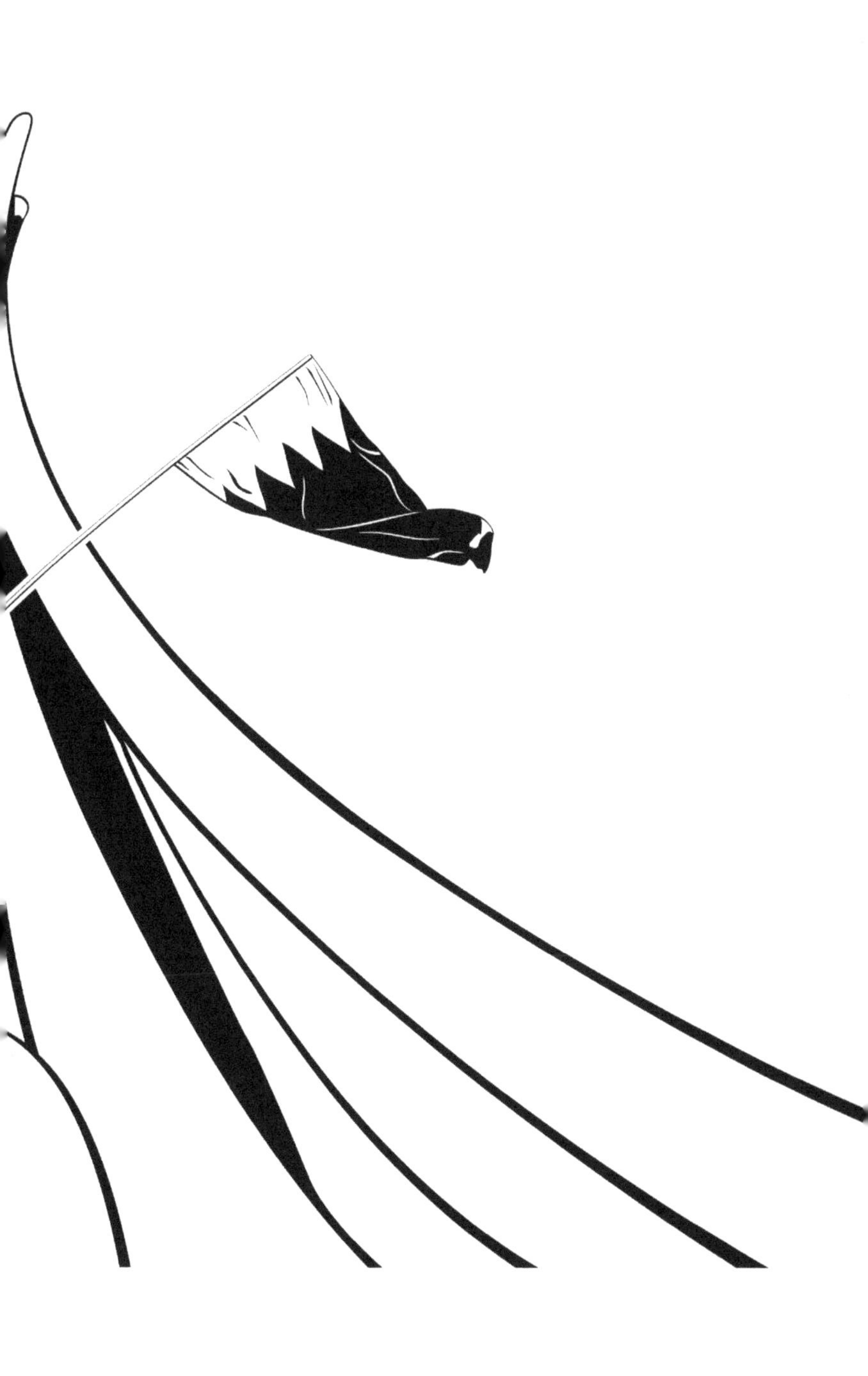

Raised Parallel

I've lived my years abroad
My heart grew parallel to a world I've barely seen
Because parallel lines never meet
Deprived of the land that has
witnessed the cries and smiles
Of those who raised me
Raised between the stories and the tales of back home
Eventually grown from their seeds
I am like many others; I have a mother, a father
But my country has orphaned me
Deprived me of seeing its sunset descend
to the corner of my eyes
And taste the fruit grown from underneath its unseen skies
My country is still beyond beautiful
Even from behind this window of separation
It is beautiful and pearls cannot compare
To the hearts that sat around its open square
Beating in unison on the fourteenth day
A day unlike the 8000 that have plagued my 22 years
A day that has opened my heart
To a wound that has followed me here
On the back of tears hidden in years gone by
Flooding old rivers
Creating new streams
Flooding the land of my dreams

While others wake up to the intermittent
songs of morning birds
They awaken to the broken cry of a
mother that has lost her son
While others see tranquil castles in the sky
and tap-tap rain on window sills
They see poisoned clouds that descend
upon their houses and bullet shells
Death finds them whether on their feet
Or inside their homes
The face of evil manifests every night
And I lay here climbing in and out of my nightmares
Knowing my flesh and blood burns
hundreds of miles away
Young faces hidden like rare birds
Only to be seen through cages
Hidden
Because you can only hide beauty
Never erase it
And they are beautiful
The blood red rose within my heart shall
never wilt whether in bud or open

Counting each day gone by that I could have spent
smelling the soil that has raised my parents
And raised me parallel

Taher Adel
01/12/2011

Orphan

Keep going dear child
Open the windows of your dreams
And fly despite the cracks in your wings
Cover the wounds of yesterday
With the garments of today
And ignite the fire of tomorrow
Know that your smile
Still quenches your mother's heart
Though angels are the only messengers
Know that your tears
Are worth more than any child
And still carve me
Like rivers carve out canyons
Dry them with your own
Because my hands seize to be
Though my heart plays its symphony
Never look down
Because your eyes have always been stationed high
And your feet the lowest you could be
So blow away the trails of dust
And pave your hope between the dead vines you see
Shield yourself from the world
Because the world was unkind to me
Leap past its lies and trickery
Know it's not worth your soul

Nor worth the tears that trickle free
But don't be afraid when your time comes to be
Because this earth is just a maze
You'll find me when you find yourself
So have you? Yes?
Then you have finally found home

Taher Adel
5/8/2011

Who Am I?

Who are you that two seas fall beneath your feet?
Who are you to sit upon a throne you have never owned?
Who are you to break pearls and hide
between their oyster homes?
Who are you that claims to be king
but knows not his people?
Who are you to scald your name upon my freedom?
Who are you to carve golden memories,
moulded upon our backs?
Who are you to set me alight and
watch while I slowly burn?
Who are you to own the letters and
words that form my thought?
Who are you to have an army at my door
step, who am I to reply with a rose?

Who am I?
Who am I for tears to quench an eye not mine?
Who am I with tears cascading off innocent cheeks?
Who am I to hide between the sun and
your shadow, afraid of both?
Who am I to offer my breath when
you've left me none to share?
Who am I to pray to the skies when
I've been deprived of land?

Who am I to paint you in white when
you've painted me in red?

Who am I to weave questions into words?
Hoping my voice will sink right in
Deep down to your very core
Asking you once more
Who is the king and who is the slave?
Who are you and who am I?

Taher Adel
28/04/2011

ABC

A Beautiful Child
Yet my eye searches to see
Who laughed, who smiled
Any show of compassion for me

Deprived for Ever, Forever
The day you left my island of dreams
As I search wherever, whenever
For you, my double 'meem'

Growing Hungry Inside
Not for the sweetness of food
But for love denied
That was never renewed

I Journey for Known Love
As the world plays together
To find what I'm undeserving of
That you call a mother

A Motherless Nocturnal Orphan
Is what is written on the script
By the tip of destiny's pen
That this orphan failed to grip

A Person Quietly Restricted
Unheard by the worlds politics
From happiness simply evicted
Because one bully chose to kick

Slaughtered Then Unfurled
Despite my simple frame
Into the evil of our world
Like wood in a flame

A Vain Xerox of Youth
Like a sealess shore
Living a lie yet truth
In a sunless day, forevermore

However through pain came the promise of Zest
And that's how one orphan learnt his Alphabet

Taher Adel
04/04/2009

Final Moments

Do you ever think what your final thoughts would be?
The final words you utter before that final breath
Whether you even know that round the corner from you
Sitting quietly across from you, sits your death
Do you ever think who might be
the final person you meet
Or the final the embrace you feel
Do you ever have any regrets
Of all the moments you wasted until that final breath?

Taher Adel
31/10/2017

Beyond All Things Rare

What is the secret of his soul?
That we flock to him to mourn and greet
When forty days becomes our goal
And life or death, for him, makes sweet
What is the secret of the shrines?
That my spirit helplessly bends
And my heart burns in sacrifice
But for the pain has sweet amends
What is the secret of this embrace?
That ignites my heart; a gentle light
Distance shall not rob me of his grace
From home, I walk forth day and night
What is the secret of the spoken songs?
That echo his story, through a melody
With trembling hearts that have no tongues
Beating along to the tragic eulogy
What is the secret of the saddened heart?
Defined by two mourning eyes
A blazing fire if it was painted art
Or a darkened cloud dropped by the skies
What is the secret of the crying pilgrims?
Straining forward on their knees
Like plotted flowers, gentle hymns
Echoing beneath the breeze
What is the secret of this universal link?

Where millions of hearts are annually pledged
From his love they all strive to drink
Returning home fully fledged
What is the secret of the enshrined sun?
A painted beauty that you cannot compare
Stars glistened and shined but failed to outdo
The beauty we flock to
Beyond all things rare.

Taher Adel
2008

I Saw Nothing But Beauty

Beneath the countless stars that sleep
in the sheets of cloudless nights
Beneath the wounded skies that hide
between the darkness and all its height
Beneath the collapsed sun, now a
shade when once it was bright
Beneath the battle fought between sunset and sunrise
And all the colours that merge and
melt to form the horizon's light
Beneath the bleeding veils that separate
the loved, eye from eye
Beneath the quiet footprints in the
sand, walking, silent scars
Beneath the shadows where petals fall
and the winds pick them up
Beneath the chains that wrestle time
until they succumb to rust
Beneath the skin that breaks and bones that shake
Beneath the flesh that aches and heart that bakes
Beneath it all
I saw nothing but beauty…

Taher Adel
16/11/2013

He Never Dies

From the land of men
Angels admired only a few
Not many were worthy of visits
Let alone a caravan of pilgrims
For a human heart was human
Beating on a whim
Unlike his
A heart caught between the crossfires
Of heaven and earth
The earth was slanted
Burning with the evil of the world
While heaven was uprooted
To settle beneath his dust
As he stood alone
Casting his shadow
Between the flames
Calling to the world
For he is the voice of justice
Written on the specks of time
Usurping our hearts
Seizing our souls
Only to mesmerise
Revolution is the earnest student of his stand
Sacrifice is his fledgling apprentice

While death is the naïve infant chasing behind
As he never dies

Taher Adel
03/12/2011

The Pledge

It's that time of year
Where the clocks pause
Like the calm before the storm
And nothing else matters
But him and his call
We leave everything aside
As if we've been called into war
Where our old lives are stripped
And left at the door
Men of young and men of old
Uniform
Unified by him and his call

Like pearls surfacing to the shore
To a place where the spirit's compass points
And every direction towards him is North
With millions of tongues replying to his call
And the feet stampeding through land and through walls
Time, space and the mysteries between them all
It's as if time itself was choking
The moment that sword was raised
As a result the years remain broken
And his call was left for eternity unscathed
So every year his banner is once again waved
And the orbit begins to the sun once again

Our feet walk, leaving our lives where they are
Our eyes face the direction of his courtyard
And our heartbeats are tied and chained
To one another, in sync and restrained
To a master enslaved
Like the many servants, both seen and unseen
Men and children in white, black and green
Feeding the world like a well oiled machine
Just like us, angels above us convene
And Death is a friend in many a journey
And at times you'd even see him smiling
When a man draws his final breath
And not long ago he pledged allegiance in crying

We come to him tear swept, sun swept and windswept
On wings and on waves
Millions of faces plotted like grains
Angels look in envy and the dead cry in the graves
As we walk towards him
In all colours and shades
As if we are weaving a rainbow of meaning
Rising from the ashes, like a phoenix in grieving
There is no sunset nor sunrise

The night is our past
And our future his shrine

Taher Adel
20/10/2017

A Lonely Grave

I glanced upon each forgotten grave
And pondered about the souls beneath the soil
One stood out, masked by scented silence
She was buried last night by a man
Who appeared to age throughout the burial
I watched on as I saw him stare into the
wounds that clawed her soul away
Carefully giving back what seemed to be
the most significant part of him
I watched how his mortal eyes stitched the
painful images left by her demise
And witnessed how her memory, once a reality
Became a secret spinning across the quilted fabrics of time
What did he find when he pressed
his fingers between her ribs?
What possessed this man to leave with her half his soul?
Tied between the soil and her lips

Dawn made an entrance accompanied by its brightness
But sunlight stopped at her grave
As if needing an invitation
Leaving it in darkness
It was a lonely grave and I couldn't help but ask
Who she was and what was the broken secret inside
I spoke to her grave one night
Her grave spoke back to me

And said
"Understand that radiant energy
Is found in us, everywhere around us
But it is not from us
Understand that she once crossed our orbit
And from her twelve sparks formed
Understand that she is an imitation
of the Sun that bore her
A reflected bride to the moon
Understand
That she walked on the earth blinding the eyes of angels
Like her father at noon
Understand that she was raised in the arms of the book
While her father was raised in hers
A mother to her father
And what was broken
Was her ribs and what was hidden was
her husband's crying heart
For who-else can bare his sadness but her?"

Taher Adel
04/04/2012

He Never Died

From the land of men
Angels admired only a few
Not many were worthy of visits
Let alone a caravan of pilgrims
For a human heart was human
Beating on a whim
Unlike his
A heart caught between the crossfires
Of heaven and earth
The earth was slanted
Burning with the evil of the world
While heaven was uprooted
To settle beneath his dust
As he stood alone
Casting his shadow
Between the flames
Calling to the world
For he is the voice of justice
Written on the specks of time
Usurping our hearts
Seizing our souls
Only to mesmerise
Revolution is the earnest student of his stand
Sacrifice is his fledgling apprentice

While death is the naïve infant chasing behind
As he never dies

Taher Adel
03/12/2011

I Am

I am the bitter story dying to be told
I am the symphony playing to your
yearning heart calling it home
Come out of your corpse and bleed with me once more
Look away from the cracked mirror of your world
Settle your eyes on the images transcending time
No need to rehearse your tears for they will find their way
As they travel through the path of my ten nights and days
I express myself through the sadness of the voices
I plant myself in poetry, sowing my seeds with every verse
My ink is the screams of those angels orbiting earth
Infecting paper like venom's deathly whisper in the veins
Hunting words and placing them on
the throne of surrendered hearts
Crowning peasants and toppling tyrants all in one breath
I am the hieroglyphs in the minds of revolutionaries
When they stand outnumbered his
memory gives them strength
I am the question of the riddle asked by the spears
I am its answer hidden beneath his eye filled tears
I am the room divided by days accepting his guests
For Fatima I am the house of sorrow built
I am the season that flowers bend and wilt
In his love eternally
I am the yearly water that will quench his thirst

Tearing the barriers between the
metaphysical and physical earth
What is philosophy when a tear is worth
an ocean in another realm?
What is love that it finds itself manifested in tears?
I am the envy of the days as I carry
his memory within my arms
Just as the moon found himself lucky that day
Under the mazes of nightfall lost in the land of Karbala
Torn between reflecting the sun or the son of Ali
For what surface is as bright as the surface of his heart?
And what day can transcend the years like his?
I am Ashurah.

Taher Adel
27/11/2011

Deep Inside This Poet's Heart

Deep inside this poet's heart
Is a world that is seldom seen
A place where pen meets paper
Where hope meets his dreams

His hopes are tied to the wind
While his dreams have slept a while
His hopes to see his nation rise
While his dream is to see the awaited smile

Deep inside this poet's heart
Is a garden struggling to survive
With leaves drifting aimlessly to the ground
And bees searching for their long lost hive

Place a rock upon his chest
For the wind might blow him away
Away from the path of the one he must find
Into his brightest night and darkest day

Deep inside this poet's heart
Is a book you cannot put down
It is hand-crafted by fading freedom
And written to the final crown

When the air is thin at the edge of night
His presence in his heart serenades him
His patience keeps him hopeful
When the leash of life overtakes him

Deep inside this poet's heart
Is a flame that shall never subside
In the dim light of evermore
Lighten for the bearer, his soul is tied

No ruler can dent his dreams
No king can drag him this deep
No leader can lead his heart
But if you're reading; it's all yours to keep

Deep inside this poet's heart
An oath written, breathed and sworn
Is a pledge he has made to Him
When pen meets paper a poem is born

Taher Adel
05/07/2011

Lightning Source UK Ltd.
Milton Keynes UK
UKHW03f0053260418
321677UK00001B/6/P

9 781546 291541